I0477864

ASHTON KUTCHER

The Multi-Talented Star-The Actor, Entrepreneur, and Philanthropist

Mary R. Wall

Ashton Kutcher

TABLE OF CONTENT

INTRODUCTION

Few people more than Ashton Kutcher exemplify the spirit of adaptability and creativity in a time when the distinctions between entertainment, technology, and social activism are becoming increasingly hazy. He was born Christopher Ashton Kutcher in Cedar Rapids, Iowa, on February 7, 1978. He has moved smoothly across the worlds of successful business endeavors, influential philanthropy, and Hollywood stardom. This in-depth biography explores the complex life of Ashton Kutcher, following his rise from a small-town childhood to international recognition for his contributions to society and technology in addition to his on-screen persona.

With his depiction of the endearing Michael Kelso on the popular comedy "That '70s Show," Kutcher first gained international recognition because of his hilarious timing and indisputable charm. His popularity on the program led to a string of high-profile parts in hit films like "Dude, Where's My Car?" and "No Strings Attached," proving that he was a versatile actor with a flair for both comedy and drama. But Kutcher had goals that went well beyond the big screen.

In the background, Kutcher was building a solid reputation as a computer enthusiast and astute investor. He was a founding partner of A-Grade Investments, a venture capital firm, and made early investments in companies like Spotify, Uber, Airbnb, and Airbnb that would go on to become household names. His reputation as a significant figure in the tech sector has been cemented by his acute sense of innovation and ability to predict market trends. Silicon Valley and Hollywood have benefited greatly from Kutcher's commitment to advancing innovative ideas and commercial savvy.

But Ashton Kutcher's steadfast dedication to philanthropy and social problems is what makes him stand out. Inspired by his own experiences and a strong sense of empathy, he co-founded Thorn, an organization that fights child sex trafficking and human trafficking. Through Thorn, Kutcher demonstrates his commitment to utilizing power for the greater good by utilizing technology to safeguard vulnerable people. Beyond his accomplishments in entertainment and business, he has gained respect and appreciation for his advocacy efforts, which have not only increased awareness but also brought about real change.

The numerous facets of Ashton Kutcher's life and work are examined in this book, including his early years in Iowa, his ascent to fame in Hollywood, his ground-breaking financial ventures, and his ceaseless charitable end endeavors Usingterviews, firsthand accounts, and meticulous examination, readers will get a comprehensive comprehension of the motivations behind this exceptional person. The life of Ashton Kutcher is a monument to the strength of fortitude, creativity, and empathy; it shows that one individual can truly have a significant impact in a variety of areas

CHAPTER 1:WHO IS ASHTON KUTCHER

Ashton Kutcher is an American entrepreneur, philanthropist, actor, and producer. His portrayal of Michael Kelso on the comedy "That '70s Show" (1998–2006) brought him initial notoriety. In addition, Kutcher has acted in severally, including "No Strings Attached" (2011), "Just Married" (2003), and "Dude, Where's My Car?" (2000). In addition, he was the creator and host of the MTV prank show "Punk'd".

In addition to his career as an actor, Kutcher is a successful venture capitalist. He co-founded A-Grade Investments, an investment firm through which he has made investments in profitable startups, such as Uber and Airbnb. In addition, he co-founded Thorn, an org organization that fights technology-based child sex exploitation and human trafficking.

Ashton Kutcher

In Cedar Rapids, Iowa, on February 7, 1978, Kutcher was born. He is currently married to actress Mila Kunis, with whom he has two daughters, after having previously been married to actress Demi Moore.

Childhood and upbringing

Christopher Ashton Kutcher, the father of Ashton Kutcher, was born in Cedar Rapids, Iowa, on February 7, 1978. As the son of factory worker Larry Kutcher and Procter & Gamble employee Diane Finnegan Kutcher, he was raised in a modest home. Kutcher has an older sister named Tausha and a fraternal twin brother named Michael. Michael, his twin brother, got a heart transplant at an early age after being born with cerebral palsy; this event had a profound impact on Kutcher and his philosophy on life.

Ashton Kutcher

Kutcher's early years were characterized by both unusual difficulties and an average Midwesterner upbringing. He went to church, played sports, and engaged in school activities—all activities that are customary for a child in Iowa. Raised in a Roman Catholic family, he completed his high school education at Cedar Rapids Washington before moving with his family to the nearby town of Tiffin, where he attended Clear Creek Amana High School.

When Kutcher was sixteen years old, his parents got divorced, which was a trying time for him. He has talked about how his brother's illness and his parents' divorce affected his mental health, acknowledging that as a teenager he experienced depression and a sense of helplessness. But he also developed a strong sense of perseverance and determination as a result of these personal struggles.

Despite these difficulties, Kutcher was well-liked for his gregarious demeanor and sense of humor in addition to his academic excellence. He participated in theatre and sports, among other extracurricular activities. His participation in school plays and his love of performing during his high school years ignited his passion for acting. But it wasn't an easy road to fame for him.

In 1996, Kutcher enrolled at the University of Iowa to study biochemical engineering following his high school graduation. His desire to find a treatment for his brother's heart disease played a role in his decision to explore this subject. Kutcher worked a variety of jobs while attending college, such as sweeping floors at a General Mills cereal facility and being a summer hire at the Cedar Rapids Blood Centre. He also joined the Delta Chi fraternity while in school.

After a talent scout saw Kutcher at an Iowa City pub, his life took a sharp change. He was persuaded to participate in the "Fresh Faces of Iowa" modeling competition. After winning, he left college to focus on his modeling career. His path into the entertainment sector began with this decision.

Ashton Kutcher

After relocating to New York City, Kutcher joined a modeling agency and soon became successful, gaining roles in advertisements and prominent companies like Calvin Klein. He traveled to Paris and Milan as part of his modeling career, where he improved his technique and gained self-assurance in front of the camera.

To pursue acting, Kutcher relocated to Los Angeles in 1998. After going to several different auditions, he quickly got the part that made him famous—that of Michael Kelso on the Fox comedy "That '70s Show." After eight seasons of great success, the program made Kutcher a household figure. His depiction as the endearing but dim-witted Kelso demonstrated his comedic skill and charm, gaining him a devoted following and international notoriety.

Ashton Kutcher's early upbringing and background had a big influence on who he would become during these crucial years. Growing up in Iowa, facing obstacles in his family, and navigating the early phases of his career left him with a strong work ethic, perseverance, and a drive for success. These traits would come in handy as he developed from a small-town boy to a successful businessman and Hollywood star.

Early life and upbringing

The experiences that created Ashton Kutcher's character and profession are woven together in a complex tapestry during his youth and upbringing. Born Christopher Ashton Kutcher on February 7, 1978, in Cedar Rapids, Iowa, he was raised in a close-knit, middle-class household that valued hard work. Despite the difficulties they encountered, his parents, Larry Kutcher, a manufacturing worker, and Diane Finnegan Kutcher, a Procter & Gamble employee, offered a secure and encouraging atmosphere.

As a child, Ashton grew up with his elder sister Tausha and his fraternal twin brother Michael. Although the birth of the twins was an important moment in the family's history, Michael's early health issues made their lives more complicated. Michael had a heart transplant when he was quite little and had cerebral palsy from birth. The Kutcher family was greatly impacted by these health issues, particularly Ashton, who at an early age showed a strong sense of empathy and accountability.

With its small-town routines and pastimes, Ashton's boyhood in Cedar Rapids was typical of a childhood in the Midwest. The family was reared as Roman Catholics, and religion was a significant part of their everyday existence. After his family moved, Ashton attended Cedar Rapids Washington High School before transferring to Clear Creek Amana High School in Tiffin. The family moved in part to get Michael better support and medical attention.

Ashton's school day consisted of both academics and extracurriculars. He played sports with enthusiasm, with a focus on football and wrestling in particular. He was well-liked by his colleagues due to his gregarious demeanor and inherent charm, and he was well-known for his sense of humor and entertainment skills. But his adolescence was also characterized by a great deal of unrest and difficulties. Emotional and psychological challenges were brought on by the strain of his brother's health problems and his parents' eventual divorce when he was sixteen. In the face of his family's hardships, Ashton has been candid about his battles with depression during this time. He was overwhelmed by a sense of helplessness.

Ashton achieved success in both his social and scholarly endeavors despite these personal struggles. He became passionate about performing, took part in school plays, and found comfort and expression in acting. His early theatre experiences gave him a creative outlet and a window into his future profession. His confidence and talent as a performer were greatly enhanced by these encounters.

Ashton's route appeared to lean towards a traditional career after high school. In 1996, he enrolled at the University of Iowa to pursue a biochemical engineering degree. Seeking treatment for his brother's cardiac ailment motivated him to pursue his studies, underscoring his strong ties to his family and feeling of responsibility. To support himself while attending university, Ashton matched his academics with several jobs. He was employed as a summer hire at the Cedar Rapids Blood Centre, cleaning floors at a General Mills cereal facility and serving as a caretaker. He developed a strong work ethic and learned the value of endurance from these occupations.

When a talent scout saw Ashton at an Iowa City pub, his life took an abrupt turn. He was persuaded to participate in the "Fresh Faces of Iowa" modeling competition, and after winning, the stage was prepared for his debut in the entertainment business. This turning point in his life caused him to leave college and relocate to New York City to pursue a modeling career.

Ashton joined a modeling agency in New York and became successful right away. His attractive features and captivating personality brought him high-profile jobs,

Ashton Kutcher

such as commercial appearances and Calvin Klein campaigns. His modeling profession introduced him to the world of show business and allowed him to visit major international fashion cities like Paris and Milan.

Ashton made a seamless transition from modeling to acting after relocating to Los Angeles to seek career chances in cinema and television. His breakout performance on the Fox comedy "That '70s Show" as Michael Kelso propelled him to stardom by showing his comic skill and winning over a large audience.

Ashton Kutcher had a unique blend of everyday Midwestern life and remarkable personal struggles during his early years. His early life lessons of perseverance, hard effort, and empathy prepared the way for his diverse career combining entertainment, business, and philanthropy. His trip from Cedar Rapids to Hollywood serves as an example of the transformational potential of tenacity and the overcoming of obstacles to follow one's passions.

CHAPTER 2: ACTING CAREER

Ashton Kutcher's acting career is evidence of his performance appeal and versatility. His portrayal of Michael Kelso on the hit sitcom "That '70s Show," which ran from 1998 to 2006, was the reason he first became well-known. Kutcher won over viewers with his endearing yet simple-minded depiction of Kelso, which also highlighted his comedic timing. He became well-known in the entertainment business as a result of this job, which also provided him with many chances.

After becoming successful on "That '70s Show," Kutcher made the move to the big screen, where he starred in several films that demonstrated the breadth of his acting abilities. His comedic abilities were further showcased in romantic comedies including "Dude, Where's My Car?" (2000), "Just Married" (2003), and "What Happens in

Vegas" (2008). But Kutcher didn't stop at comedy; he also tried his hand at tragic parts. The science fiction psychological thriller "The Butterfly Effect," which he appeared in in 2004, gave him the chance to show off his ability to handle more difficult and serious material.

A combination of critically praised roles and box office successes can be seen throughout Kutcher's filmography. Among his noteworthy cinematic credits are the comedies "Guess Who" (2005) and "No Strings Attached" (2011), in which he starred opposite Natalie Portman. Even with unfavorable reviews for a few of his films, Kutcher's career as a bankable Hollywood star endured.

When Kutcher replaced Charlie Sheen in the cast of the popular sitcom "Two and a Half Men," in 2011, he made a big comeback to television. Kutcher's portrayal of the eccentric billionaire Walden Schmidt served to rejuvenate the show, which benefited from high viewership until its cancellation in 2015. His position as

Ashton Kutcher

a prominent character in television humor was further cemented by this performance.

In addition, Kutcher has looked into opportunities off-camera. He served as an executive producer for the MTV reality show "Punk'd," which he created and hosted. The show, which featured pulling elaborate practical jokes on famous people, was a huge hit and ran for multiple seasons until going viral in the early 2000s. His production firm, Katalyst Films, has worked on several projects that demonstrate his aptitude and enthusiasm for producing and creating original material.

Kutcher has been involved in streaming platform roles more lately. In the Netflix series "The Ranch" (2016–2020), for example, he played the central character, a former semi-pro football player who returns to assist in running the family ranch. With this comedy-drama hybrid, Kutcher was able to showcase his adaptability and audience engagement in a variety of settings.

Ashton Kutcher

Ashton Kutcher has demonstrated during his acting career that he is a multi-talented celebrity who can give memorable and enjoyable performances. His transformation from a comedy hottie to a well-respected actor and producer highlights his capacity to adjust and grow in the constantly shifting entertainment world.

Change to Television

Ashton Kutcher's move to television was a turning point in his career, as his prominence and influence in the entertainment business increased thanks to calculated decisions and standout performances. Kutcher was first noticed for his comedic abilities on the small screen, and his comeback to television solidified his reputation as an adaptable actor who could work in a variety of genres.

In 2011, Kutcher made his biggest comeback to television when he was cast in the hit sitcom "Two and a Half Men." Since he was taking over for Charlie Sheen, whose exit from the show was widely reported and contentious, this move was audacious as well as dangerous. Walden Schmidt, a millionaire internet entrepreneur with an oddball and sometimes gullible demeanor, was portrayed by Kutcher. His character's dynamic differed from Sheen's, providing a fresh vitality to the show. Fans reacted favorably to Kutcher's portrayal, and he was successful in keeping the show's high ratings, which attracted a sizable audience until the end of the series in 2015.

In addition to reviving Kutcher's career on television, "Two and a Half Men" demonstrated his versatility in fitting into well-known genres and adding his distinct charm to adored shows. He was praised for his portrayal of Walden Schmidt, which brought humor and a hint of sensitivity to the character, making it both amusing and realistic. Kutcher's role in the show's latter seasons proved to be a crucial factor in its sustained popularity, showcasing his ability to anchor a big network series.

Ashton Kutcher

In the television industry, Kutcher has had a significant impact not just as an actor but also as a producer. Among his most significant accomplishments was the MTV prank show "Punk'd," which he produced and wrote. "Punk'd" gained popularity after its 2003 premiere and was well-known for its intricate practical jokes on famous people. As the show's host and mastermind, Kutcher demonstrated his inventiveness and sense of humor, which enhanced his standing as a significant player in television production. The success of the show resulted in several seasons and revivals, demonstrating both Kutcher's talent for crafting compelling content and its continuing appeal.

Through his participation in streaming services, Kutcher has continued to investigate prospects in the television industry. In 2016, he landed a major part in the Netflix original series "The Ranch." Kutcher skillfully balanced comedy and emotion in his portrayal as Colt Bennett, a former semi-pro football player who returns to his family's Colorado ranch. "The Ranch" showcased Kutcher's ability to play complex roles by allowing him to explore more intricate storylines and character development. Over its four seasons, the program developed a devoted following and proved Kutcher's popularity in the rapidly changing digital streaming market.

Kutcher's move to television is another example of his deeper comprehension of the media environment and his aptitude for utilizing many channels to connect with a wide range of viewers. His participation in several telseveralws demonstrates his versatility as a talent and business sense, both in front of and behind the camera. Kutcher's capacity to adapt and look forward is demonstrated by his successful navigating of the television industry, especially at a time when the emergence of streaming services has brought about substantial change.

In summary, Ashton Kutcher's move to television is marked by calculated decisions that have helped him to gain more clout and demonstrate his versatility as an actor and producer. From bringing a big network comedy back to life to developing and producing ground-breaking reality TV and landing key parts in streaming shows, Kutcher has continuously shown that he can entertain and engage viewers in a variety of forms. His work on television not only demonstrates his skill and originality but also his awareness of the changing media landscape and his ability to flourish in it.

Current and Future Initiatives

Ashton Kutcher has been performing, producing, and investing in creative content in addition to broadening his portfolio in recent years. His strategy shows a keen interest in current media trends and a dedication to investigating uncharted territory in the entertainment sector.

A noteworthy recent endeavor for Kendeavors is the Netflix series "The Ranch," which aired from 2016 until

Ashton Kutcher

2020. In the television series, Kutcher portrayed Colt Bennett, a former football player in the semi-pro ranks who comes back to assist in running his family's ranch in Colorado. The comedy and drama elements of "The Ranch" gave Kutcher thallowed Kutcher nuanced and experienced character. The show garnered positive reviews, especially for its accurate depiction of rural American life and the intricacies of family relationships. Kutcher showed that he could handle a more serious and emotionally charged role with his performance, which was hailed for its depth and relatability.

In addition to "The Ranch," Kutcher has worked on several other projects that make use of his production experience and spirit of entrepreneurship. He is still active through Katalyst Films, his production firm, which has been crucial in developing and generating material that appeals to contemporary audiences. Even while Katalyst frequently withholds specifics of new projects until formal announcements, the company's history points to an emphasis on creative and compelling material.

Ashton Kutcher

Additionally, Kutcher has been more involved in the streaming and digital media industries. His passion for these fields complements his larger entrepreneurial endeavors, especially his investments in early-stage technological companies. Because of the synergy between his tech investments and entertainment career, Kutcher can contribute a distinct viewpoint to the content he creates, frequently fusing cutting-edge technology with modern themes.

One impending endeavor that aroused a lot of excitement is Kutcher's role in the biopic "The Long Home." The film, which is based on the same-titled novel by William Gay, was directed by James Franco. The plot is about a young man who unintentionally works for the bootlegger who killed his father in rural Tennessee in the 1940s. In contrast to his typical romantic and humorous parts, Kutcher's role in this movie gives him the chance to explore more dramatic and nuanced character work. With such a great cast and intriguing source material, the project is much awaited.

Ashton Kutcher

Furthermore, Kutcher has demonstrated a strong interest in initiatives that tackle social concerns and have a significant influence. His continued involvement with Thorn: Digital Defenders of Children, an organization he and Demi Moore co-founded, is indicative of this. Thorn focuses on creating technological tools to fight child sex abuse and human trafficking. As part of his commitment to this subject, Kutcher has spoken before Congress and supported improvements to laws that will better protect disadvantaged groups. His collaboration with Thorn demonstrates his dedication to using his platform for social good, even though it is not a conventional entertainment endeavor.

In addition to his current and planned endeavors, Kutcher has made several media and broadcast appearances that showcase his knowledge and viewpoints on entrepreneurship, technology, and social issues. He frequently speaks on his investments, the direction of technology, and his charitable endeavors in panels, podcasts, and interviews. His continued

Ashton Kutcher

prominence and importance in the tech and entertainment sectors are aided by these appearances.

To sum up, Ashton Kutcher has a dynamic and diverse approach to his business, which is seen in his current and prospective endeavors. From producing and acting in television shows to investing in cutting-edge material and supporting significant social issues, Kutcher is a well-known personality in the entertainment business. He will continue to be a prominent and powerful figure in the rapidly evolving media and entertainment industry thanks to his ability to adjust to new trends and make the most of his many interests and skills.

CHAPTER 3: ENTREPRENEURIAL VENTURES

With the help of his celebrity profile and astute business sense, Ashton Kutcher has made a name for himself as a formidable entrepreneur who has advanced technology and investing. His entrepreneurial path is marked by several calculated bets, joint ventures, and a strong commitment to the technology sector, all of which have greatly expanded his professional horizons and increased his profile outside of Hollywood.

In 2010, Kutcher made his debut in the business sector when he, billionaire businessman Ron Burkle, and entertainment manager Guy Oseary co-founded A-Grade Investments. A-Grade made a name for itself swiftly for spotting and supporting creative entrepreneurs. Identifying disruptive companies with the potential to revolutionize their respective industries was at the core of the firm's investment philosophy. A prominent achievement during their initial years was their investment in Airbnb, the widely used platform for short-term rentals. A-Grade recognized the potential of Airbnb's business concept while many others doubted that strangers could properly rent out their homes. The multi-billion dollar growth of Airbnb made this investment lucrative.

A-Grade Investments supported several well-known firms in addition to Airbnb, including Uber, Spotify, and Warby Parker. For Kutcher and his colleagues, Uber—the massive ride-sharing company—represented yet another noteworthy victory. Their initial investment in Uber was made at a pivotal juncture when the business was still growing and validating its concept in numerous global locations. Similarly, Spotify's ascent to prominence as a music streaming service provided additional evidence of A-Grade's ability to identify winners in the tech industry.

A-Grade Investments is only one of Kutcher's business ventures. Alongside Guy Oseary, he co-founded Sound Ventures in 2015 as an A-Grade replacement. With a more expansive scope, Sound Ventures carried on the tradition of funding early-stage technological businesses. Since then, the company has made investments in businesses in a range of industries, including consumer goods, fintech, and health tech. Companies like Bird, an electric scooter startup, and Robinhood, a stock trading website, are notable investments. Kutcher's interest in technology that has the power to democratize access and change daily life is demonstrated by these investments.

Kutcher's active involvement in the IT world and hands-on approach are contributing factors to his success as an investor. He is renowned for being eager to become hands-on involved in the businesses he invests in, frequently offering insightful commentary and using his connections to support the expansion of start-ups.

Ashton Kutcher

Beyond providing financial support, he frequently counsels businesses on product development, scalability operations, and marketing tactics. He stands out from many other celebrity investors who might play a more supportive role with this direct involvement.

In addition to investing, Kutcher has started his own businesses. One noteworthy instance is his partnership with Jason Goldberg in the development of the content production company Katalyst Media. Popular TV series like "Punk'd" and "Beauty and the Geek," created by Katalyst, showcase Kutcher's talent for crafting captivating content that connects with viewers. The entertainment industry success of the company served as a solid springboard for Kutcher's subsequent business endeavors.

Kutcher's work with Thorn: Digital Defenders of Children, an organization he co-founded with Demi Moore, is another example of his entrepreneurial zeal. Thorn creates technological solutions to stop child sex trafficking and human trafficking. Kutcher's endeavor demonstrates his dedication to using technology for social good. As part of his creative strategy, Thorn has developed software tools that make it easier for law enforcement to find and rescue victims of human trafficking. Due to his collaboration with Thorn, Kutcher has gained notoriety as a leading proponent of kid safety and the positive societal effects of technology.

Apart from his investments and charitable activities, Kutcher regularly speaks at conferences, conducts interviews, and posts on social media about technology and business. His participation in these talks contributes to a better understanding of how technology can be used to spur innovation and effect positive change by bridging the divide between Silicon Valley and Hollywood.

To sum up, Ashton Kutcher's business endeavors demonstrate a thorough and significant involvement with the technology sector. Kutcher has shown a remarkable ability to recognize and promote revolutionary ideas, from co-founding enterprises that address critical societal concerns to making early-stage investments in innovative startups. His practical approach and in-depth knowledge of media and technology have allowed him to develop a broad and prosperous portfolio. Kutcher is demonstrating that his abilities go well beyond acting by continuing to grow his influence through his business ventures.

A-Grade Investments co-founder

A major turning point in Ashton Kutcher's career occurred in 2010 when he co-founded A-Grade Investments, showcasing his aptitude for venture capital and his intense interest in the digital sector. Alongside wealthy grocery tycoon Ron Burkle and entertainment manager Guy Oseary, A-Grade Investments was founded. Together, the three sought to take advantage of the growing ecosystem of tech startups by offering access to their vast networks, strategic advice, and funding.

Ashton Kutcher

When A-Grade Investments first started, Silicon Valley
was experiencing a wave of rapid innovation, with many
entrepreneurs proposing disruptive technology and
upending established business structures. Kutcher's
sincere interest in technology and how it may change
businesses and daily life motivated him to enter this
field. Kutcher used a hands-on strategy, immersing
himself in the digital culture, attending industry events,
and interacting with entrepreneurs on a personal level, in
contrast to many celebrity investors who might only use
their notoriety as leverage.

Investing in Airbnb was one of A-Grade Investments'
first and most well-known ventures. With its innovative
idea of short-term house rentals, Airbnb was still a
relatively obscure firm at the time of the funding.
Kutcher and his partners anticipated a time when
consumers would favour individualized and affordable
housing choices over conventional hotels, realizing the
disruptive potential of Airbnb's business model in the
hospitality sector. This early investment paid off
handsomely, as Airbnb expanded to become a

multibillion-dollar business that completely changed how people travel and book lodging.

A-Grade has made a sizable investment in the massive ride-sharing company Uber. Uber's creative approach to urban transportation, which promised to make moving across cities more convenient, economical, and effective, caught Kutcher and his team's attention. Early investments in Uber paid off handsomely as the business grew internationally and rose to become one of the most valuable businesses in history. Uber's success story demonstrated how A-Grade may recognize firms that have viable mass market adoption and scalable business concepts.

Spotify, the music streaming service that revolutionized how people listen to and access music, was also supported by A-Grade Investments. Kutcher and his partners recognized the shift in consumer behavior from physical media and downloads to streaming, and they saw potential in Spotify's platform, which provided an extensive music catalog that was available for on-demand listening. The popularity of Spotify served as additional evidence for A-Grade's investment approach, which focuses on businesses that employ technology to improve user experiences.

Another noteworthy A-Grade investment was Warby Parker, the eyeglasses firm that upended the conventional retail model by selling spectacles directly to customers online. The company's creative approach to design, cost, and convenience complemented A-Grade's mission to promote companies that are revolutionizing their respective markets. The success of Warby Parker served as a testament to the growing popularity of direct-to-consumer firms and their capacity to cultivate devoted internet followings.

Kutcher did more for A-Grade Investments than just contribute money. He was actively involved in providing strategic guidance, coaching company founders, and using his public persona to garner media attention and legitimacy for the businesses that A-Grade invested in. Unlike many other celebrity investors, he is deeply involved in these ventures and genuinely interested in their success. Kutcher frequently provided operational advice, marketing tactics, and insights into product development, all of which assisted these firms in overcoming obstacles to growth and market penetration.

Another factor contributing to A-Grade Investments' success is the cooperative relationship between Burkle, Oseary, and Kutcher. Kutcher's celebrity status and tech passion, Oseary's ties in the entertainment sector and managerial know-how, and Burkle's financial ability and wide-ranging business network were all distinct advantages that each brought to the table. Because of this combination, A-Grade was able to provide businesses with a full range of benefits, including funding, strategic counsel, mentoring, and priceless networking opportunities.

The portfolio of A-Grade Investments expanded to encompass a wide range of businesses in numerous industries, demonstrating the partners' wide-ranging interests and progressive outlook. The investing philosophy of the business placed a strong emphasis on supporting visionary founders who had ground-breaking ideas that may upend well-established industries. Numerous A-Grade portfolio firms have achieved outstanding exits and values, demonstrating the effectiveness of this strategy.

In conclusion, Ashton Kutcher demonstrated his entrepreneurial zeal and his capacity to recognize and support game-changing firms by co-founding A-Grade Investments. The company's profitable investments in startups like Spotify, Airbnb, Uber, and Warby Parker demonstrated its aptitude for selecting winners in the internet industry. The success of A-Grade was largely due to Kutcher's strategic insights and active involvement, which solidified his reputation as a significant figure in the venture capital industry. By showcasing his abilities outside of acting through A-Grade Investments, Kutcher has cemented his status as a shrewd investor and visionary businessman.

Ashton Kutcher

Capital Invested in Technology Startups

Due to his investments in tech businesses, Ashton Kutcher has become a well-known name in the venture capital industry. His entry into this field started in 2010 when he, along with Guy Oseary and Ron Burkle, co-founded the venture capital firm A-Grade Investments. Kutcher's approach has always centered on finding innovative businesses that can completely transform their respective sectors. His strategy leverages his celebrity position, strategic mentoring, and financial support to help the firms he supports get more traction and legitimacy.

One of Kutcher's most well-known investments was in Airbnb, a website that allows people to rent out their houses to tourists, completely changing the hospitality sector. Kutcher and his partners invested when Airbnb was still a young company with doubts about its business plan. Kutcher recognized the possibility of a significant change in the way that people view travel accommodations. His investment and A-Grade's backing contributed to Airbnb's explosive growth, making it a multibillion-dollar business and a global household name.

An additional noteworthy investment was made in Uber, the ride-sharing platform that revolutionized urban transportation. Uber changed the game with its novel concept of using a smartphone app to match drivers and riders. Uber was growing quickly at the time Kutcher made his initial investment, but there were still a lot of regulatory obstacles to overcome. By supporting Uber, Kutcher showed that he had a sharp eye for disruptive, scalable technology that solved a prevalent issue with urban mobility. The subsequent success of Uber on a worldwide scale proved that this investment was wise.

Spotify, the music streaming platform that has revolutionized the music business, is another investment in Kutcher's portfolio. Seeing that streaming was replacing digital downloads and physical media, Kutcher invested in Spotify, which provided a sizable music library that was available whenever you wanted it. His knowledge of changing consumer behavior and the technology developments causing these changes were in line with this investment. The ascent of Spotify to prominence as one of the biggest music streaming services was evidence of Kutcher's vision and approach to investing.

The eyeglasses brand Warby Parker is another noteworthy addition to Kutcher's resume. The business was able to sell glasses online for less money than traditional shops thanks to its direct-to-consumer business strategy. By cutting out the typical retail markup and offering fashionable, reasonably priced spectacles straight to customers, Warby Parker upended the eyeglass market. Kutcher's investment in Warby Parker was a reflection of his interest in cutting-edge business strategies that use technology to provide customers with greater value and convenience.

In addition to these well-known brands, Kutcher has made investments in several other cutting-edge businesses in a range of industries. Robinhood, a stock trading platform that democratizes access to financial markets, is one example of such an investment. A large number of people signed up for Robinhood thanks to its commission-free trading strategy, especially younger investors. Given his interest in financial technology (fintech) and his conviction that technology can improve access to and equity in financial services, Kutcher's investment in Robinhood is telling.

An additional noteworthy investment is in Bird, an electric scooter business that has created a brand-new way to get around town. For quick city travels, Bird's dockless electric scooters provide an easy and sustainable substitute. Kutcher's endorsement of Bird is consistent with his larger investment ethos, which aims to encourage businesses that offer novel answers to everyday urban problems.

Health tech is one area in which Kutcher invests in tech businesses. He has made investments in businesses such as Zocdoc, an online resource that assists patients in finding physicians and scheduling visits. Kutcher is drawn to innovations that have a significant impact, like Zocdoc, which enhances healthcare services' efficiency and facilitates people's access to care. His interest in health technology is a reflection of his awareness of the vital role that technology can play in enhancing patient outcomes and healthcare delivery.

Kutcher takes a more thoughtful and non-monetary approach to investing. He is renowned for being actively involved in the businesses he invests in; frequently, he offers strategic counsel and uses his wide network to support the expansion of startups. He stands himself from many other celebrity investors because of his active involvement, which also highlights his dedication to these projects' success. In addition to providing advice on product creation, marketing tactics, and scaling operations, Kutcher regularly serves as a mentor to entrepreneurs. His ability to connect the dots between the tech and entertainment sectors gives the firms in his portfolio a distinct advantage.

Ashton Kutcher

Furthermore, Kutcher frequently reflects his values and interests in his investments. As an example, his investment in Acorns, a micro-investing program that assists users in saving and investing spare change, is consistent with his views regarding financial empowerment and literacy. In a similar vein, his endorsement of organizations that tackle social issues—like Thorn, which creates technology to fight human trafficking—evidences his dedication to using technology for good in society.

Kutcher's involvement in industry events, conferences, and panel discussions further solidifies his profile in the tech investment arena. He frequently gives talks at tech conferences where he imparts his knowledge on investing, entrepreneurship, and the direction of technology. Through these interactions, he can stay up to date on new prospects and trends while also increasing his profile within the tech world.

To sum up, Ashton Kutcher's investments in digital businesses demonstrate a thorough knowledge of the

industry and a calculated approach to venture capital.
His portfolio, which includes well-known brands like
Warby Parker, Uber, Airbnb, and Spotify, demonstrates
his capacity to recognize and back game-changing
businesses. Kutcher has proven by his active
participation and smart mentoring that his contributions
go beyond money, giving entrepreneurs the direction and
tools they require to be successful. His financial
contributions demonstrate his dedication to disruption,
innovation, and the beneficial effects of technology on
society.

CHAPTER 4: PHILANTHROPY AND ACTIVISM

As diverse and significant as his career in film and business, Ashton Kutcher's activism and philanthropy. Kutcher has shown a strong commitment to social causes via his many endeavors, using his position, connections, and power to take on some of the most important problems of the day.

The fact that Kutcher and his then-wife Demi Moore co-founded Thorn: Digital Defenders of Children in 2012 is a pillar of his charitable endeavors. A nonprofit organization called Thorn is committed to leveraging technology to stop child sex abuse and human trafficking. The company creates software solutions to aid law enforcement authorities with their investigations, disrupt online platforms that enable exploitation, and help locate and rescue victims of human trafficking. Since its launch, Thorn's main product, Spotlight, has been credited with assisting in the identification of thousands of victims and traffickers. Due to his fervent support of Thorn's cause, Kutcher has spoken before Congress, bringing attention to the issue and urging more stringent regulations to safeguard children who are at risk. His collaboration with Thorn demonstrates his dedication to using technology for social benefit and having a real influence on world problems.

Apart from his collaboration with Thorn, Kutcher has taken part in several other altruistic projects. He has contributed to groups that promote global development, health, and education. Beyond monetary donations, Kutcher frequently gets involved in campaigns and uses his notoriety to draw attention to causes close to his heart. He has, for instance, consistently backed the United Nations Foundation, especially when it comes to programs that attempt to combat poverty and advance global health. His support of the UN Foundation's initiatives demonstrates his conviction that teamwork is essential to addressing difficult global issues.

Kutcher has also demonstrated a strong interest in sustainability in the environment. He has backed and contributed to businesses and projects that advance sustainable business practices and green technologies. His collaboration with businesses like the electric scooter startup Bird is indicative of his dedication to lowering urban pollution and advancing environmentally friendly transportation options. Kutcher supports and advances sustainable technology, which advances the larger cause for climate action and environmental preservation.

A noteworthy facet of Kutcher's philanthropy is his endorsement of education and the empowerment of the young. He has volunteered for groups like Knowledge Is Power Programme (KIPP), which runs a network of public charter schools that offer impoverished communities access to top-notch instruction. Kutcher's advocacy for educational endeavors is indicative of his conviction in the transformational potential of education and the significance of granting equal opportunity to every child, irrespective of their financial status.

Kutcher also gives back to the tech industry through his charitable endeavors. Recognizing the need for more representation to spur innovation and equity, he has been a champion for greater diversity and inclusion in the tech sector. Kutcher has supported programs that help minorities and women, who are underrepresented in technology, through his financial contributions and public remarks. His goal is to make the tech business more diverse and vibrant by bringing in a wide range of talents and perspectives.

Kutcher frequently uses his social media channels to mobilize support for charitable causes and raise awareness of numerous social concerns in addition to his formal philanthropic endeavors. His sizable fan base enables him to connect with a wide audience and spark important discussions on issues like social justice, disaster aid, and mental health. Kutcher is committed to using his influence responsibly and for the greater good, as seen by his willingness to discuss these topics with his followers.

Kutcher's involvement in public campaigns and activities further demonstrates his activism. He has worked with groups like the Polaris Project and the DNA Foundation to fight human trafficking and modern slavery. Through his participation in events, speeches, and media appearances, he promotes public advocacy by emphasizing the significance of tackling these pressing concerns and inspiring others to take up the cause.

Additionally, Kutcher has demonstrated a willingness to back cutting-edge philanthropic strategies. He has worked on social enterprises and crowdfunding platforms that try to democratize giving and make it simpler for people to support causes they care about. His involvement with these platforms demonstrates his faith in the strength of group effort and the potential of technology to improve philanthropic giving.

In conclusion, Ashton Kutcher's activism and philanthropy are distinguished by a sincere and abiding desire to have a constructive influence on the world. Kutcher has shown a diverse approach to charity through his work with Thorn, his support of global health and education initiatives, his advocacy for environmental sustainability, and his attempts to advance diversity in the tech industry. His commitment to bringing about significant and long-lasting change is demonstrated by his readiness to use his connections, resources, and personal involvement in these causes. Kutcher has left behind a charitable legacy that consists of using his position for good, standing up for the weak, and supporting creative solutions to some of the most important problems facing humanity.

The Battle Against Human Trafficking

One of the most important and influential parts of Ashton Kutcher's charitable and activism activities is his fight against human trafficking. His conviction that technology can be used to solve some of the most important problems facing the world is the foundation of his dedication to this cause. Kutcher has been instrumental in creating cutting-edge instruments to combat child sexual exploitation and human trafficking since he co-founded Thorn: Digital Defenders of Children.

In 2012, Kutcher and his former spouse Demi Moore founded Thorn as a reaction to their increasing consciousness of the pervasive and catastrophic consequences of child exploitation and human trafficking. The organization's goal is to push technological innovation in the fight against child sexual abuse and to remove any content that promotes child sexual abuse from the internet. Thorn takes a multipronged approach, developing software tools, forming alliances with tech firms and law enforcement, and promoting public awareness to influence governmental changes.

Ashton Kutcher

One of Thorn's most important contributions to the battle against human trafficking is the creation of the software program Spotlight, which helps law enforcement find and rescue trafficking victims. Spotlight analyses internet data using sophisticated data analytics and machine learning to find trends that can be used to identify possible victims and traffickers. Since its launch, Spotlight has grown to be an invaluable tool for law enforcement, speeding up investigations and increasing the precision of their work. Thorn claims that thousands of victims have been identified thanks in part to Spotlight, which has also helped many traffickers be apprehended.

Beyond establishing and providing financing for Thorn, Kutcher is deeply involved with the organization. His involvement in its strategy, operations, and lobbying work is profound. He routinely gives speeches at gatherings, summits, and other public gatherings to promote Thorn's work and to increase awareness of the problem of human trafficking. When he spoke before the Senate Foreign Relations Committee in 2017 regarding the problem of modern slavery and human trafficking, it was one of his most prominent appearances. Throughout his evidence, Kutcher fervently emphasized the need to utilize technology to fight these crimes and urged increased cooperation between the public and commercial sectors.

During his evidence, Kutcher emphasized the organization's work's human impact by sharing moving accounts of victims who had been saved by Thorn's tools. He made the case that businesses must invest in technology if they want to keep up with human traffickers, who are increasingly using advanced digital techniques to take advantage of their victims. Because of Kutcher's testimony, the topic received a lot of media coverage, which aided in gaining support for anti-trafficking campaigns.

In addition to Spotlight, Thorn has created additional cutting-edge resources to address child sexual exploitation online. Safer is a software suite that assists enterprises in identifying, eliminating, and reporting child sexual abuse material (CSAM) from their platforms. With its seamless integration with current systems and use of cutting-edge technology for CSAM identification and scanning, Safer helps safeguard children who are at risk of harm and lessens the dissemination of illicit content. Thorn expands its influence beyond law enforcement to include prevention and early intervention by giving these capabilities to tech businesses.

In addition, Kutcher works to promote partnerships with governments, other non-profits, and significant-tech businesses. To combat human trafficking, Thorn has collaborated with top tech companies such as Google, Facebook, and Microsoft, utilizing their knowledge and assets. Thorn's tools have been scaled and made available to as many people as possible thanks to these partnerships. These partnerships have been made possible in large part by Kutcher's ability to unite the IT sector and social advocacy.

Ashton Kutcher

Apart from his collaboration with Thorn, Kutcher has backed several groups and projects that try to stop human trafficking. He has experience working with the Polaris Project, which runs the U.S. Support is offered to victims of human trafficking through the National Human Trafficking Hotline. Through his involvement, Kutcher has helped Polaris gain awareness and money for its vital services for survivors and to increase the efficacy of anti-trafficking laws.

The hallmarks of Kutcher's strategy against human trafficking are creativity, teamwork, and awareness-building. He thinks technology has the potential to be a positive force that can upend traffickers' operations and give law enforcement and support agencies additional resources. His practical involvement, public advocacy, and strategic attempts to develop a comprehensive response to trafficking that encompasses prevention, intervention, and assistance for survivors demonstrate his unwavering devotion to this cause.

To conclude, Ashton Kutcher's endeavors to combat human trafficking through Thorn and other projects demonstrate his strong dedication to social justice and his faith in the revolutionary potential of technology. By creating cutting-edge resources, encouraging teamwork, and increasing public awareness, Kutcher has made a substantial impact on the worldwide effort to combat child exploitation and human trafficking. In addition to saving innumerable lives, his work has established a standard for using technology to solve some of the most pressing and difficult social problems facing the globe today.

Other philanthropic endeavours

Ashton Kutcher is known for his efforts against human trafficking, but he also engages in other charity activities. He has actively participated in a wide range of charitable endeavors, lending assistance to various initiatives about global development, environmental sustainability, health, and education. His all-encompassing philanthropic strategy shows a dedication to making a beneficial impact in a variety of industries by utilizing his resources, connections, and personal involvement.

Kutcher has been a strong supporter of education as he understands how it can change people and communities. He has backed several educational projects that try to give marginalized communities access to high-quality education. His participation in KIPP (Knowledge Is Power Programme), a nationwide network of public charter schools that aims to prepare kids from low-income neighborhoods for success in college and life, is one well-known example. By supporting KIPP, Kutcher has contributed to providing students with access to high-quality education, rigorous academic programs, and extensive support services. His dedication to education stems from his conviction that all children, regardless of socioeconomic status, should have the chance to realize their full potential.

Ashton Kutcher

Apart from endorsing traditional schooling, Kutcher has also taken part in campaigns that encourage financial empowerment and literacy. His involvement with Acorns, an app that facilitates micro-investing and helps users save and manage spare change, demonstrates his commitment to the value of financial literacy. The goal of Acorns is to democratize access to the financial markets so that people, especially those with little financial experience, can more easily accumulate money over time. Kutcher's advocacy for Acorns is consistent with his overarching charitable objectives of fostering economic equity and individual empowerment.

Other fields in which Kutcher has made a major impact are health and well-being. He has been active in several organizations that work to better the health of the world and help those in need. Kutcher has backed the United Nations Foundation, especially its initiatives to combat global health issues like HIV/AIDS, malaria, and maternal health. Kutcher has contributed to efforts to save lives and enhance health outcomes in some of the most vulnerable areas in the world by supporting and endorsing the UN Foundation.

Additionally, Kutcher has demonstrated a significant dedication to environmental sustainability. He has backed and contributed to businesses that advance environmentally friendly procedures and innovations. His participation with Bird, an electric scooter firm that provides an eco-friendly transit option in cities, is one noteworthy example. Bird's dockless electric scooters are an eco-friendly and practical way to travel that aims to lessen carbon emissions and traffic congestion. Kutcher's investment in Bird is indicative of his commitment to advancing a greener future and developing creative solutions to environmental problems.

Apart from his investments, Kutcher has also utilized his position to advocate for environmental causes. He has taken part in public debates and campaigns to persuade people and companies to embrace sustainable practices. Kutcher is a strong proponent of environmental sustainability because he recognizes how critical it is to combat climate change and save natural resources for the next generations.

Kutcher also supports humanitarian aid and disaster relief in his charitable endeavors. He has contributed to and generated money for charities that aid areas hit by natural disasters and humanitarian emergencies. His involvement frequently entails rallying his fan base and using his social media following to raise money for humanitarian aid initiatives. By doing this, Kutcher contributes to making sure that vital resources are sent to those in need during emergencies.

In addition to his monetary gifts, Kutcher regularly participates in charitable events and advocates for causes in the public sphere. To encourage others to take action and to promote the topics he cares about, he routinely talks and attends summits, conferences, and fundraisers. His prominence and clout in the entertainment sector enable him to draw substantial attention to a range of social issues, so enhance thus the effectiveness of his charitable endeavors.

Ashton Kutcher

Another aspect of Kutcher's philanthropic strategy is its emphasis on collaborations and collaboration. He is aware that solving complicated societal issues calls for teamwork and cooperation between many sectors. Kutcher frequently collaborates with non-profits, business partners, and other philanthropists to increase the effect of his humanitarian projects. This kind of working together makes the projects he backs more successful and encourages a larger movement for constructive social change.

In conclusion, Ashton Kutcher's humanitarian activities span a variety of topics and demonstrate his strong desire to change the world for the better. Kutcher has made a wide range of varied and impactful charitable contributions, including helping to advance financial literacy, education, and global health as well as environmental sustainability and disaster relief. His strategy tackles some of the most important social concerns of the day by combining financial contributions, public campaigning, and tactical alliances.

Ashton Kutcher

Kutcher shows via his charitable endeavors that his impact goes well beyond the entertainment and business sectors, positively impacting innumerable people's lives as well as the communities in which they reside.

CHAPTER 5: PERSONAL LIFE

Like his career, Ashton Kutcher's personal life has been full of facets and energy. Born Christopher Ashton Kutcher on February 7, 1978, in Cedar Rapids, Iowa, he was raised in a middle-class household alongside his older sister Tausha and twin brother Michael. After receiving a heart transplant, Michael, who had cerebral palsy from birth, had a tremendous shift in his perspective on life and his sense of duty to his family.

Before going to Clear Creek Amana High School, Kutcher attended Washington High School in Cedar Rapids. He participated in school plays during his high school years, demonstrating an early passion for acting. But when he enrolled at the University of Iowa to study biochemical engineering, his career path changed. His desire to discover a treatment for his brother's cardiac disease drove him to pursue this profession. To pay for his tuition while attending college, Kutcher took on a variety of tasks, such as selling his plasma and cleaning floors at a General Mills facility.

When a talent scout saw Kutcher at an Iowa City bar, his life took a dramatic turn. He entered and won the "Fresh Faces of Iowa" modeling competition as a result of this interaction, and he was offered a contract with a modeling agency as well as a trip to New York City. His acting career began when his modeling job gained him access to the entertainment sector.

Kutcher was well-known for his high-profile romances during his formative years. Actress Demi Moore and he started dating in 2003, and in 2005 they got married. Moore, who is 15 years older than Kutcher, and Moore's age difference contributed to the considerable media attention their relationship received. They were viewed as a Hollywood power couple despite the criticism, frequently showing up together at public events and in advertisements. But in 2013, their marriage broke down, and the divorce was officially formalized the following year.

After parting ways with Moore, Kutcher started dating actress Mila Kunis, who was once his co-star on "That '70s Show." Their real-life chemistry was matched on screen, and they went on to become one of Hollywood's most popular pairs. In October of the same year, Wyatt Isabelle, the couple's first child, was born. The pair got engaged in February 2014. They tied the knot in a secret ceremony in July 2015. Their second child, a son named Dimitri Portwood, was born in November 2016. Kutcher and Kunis are renowned for maintaining a low profile in the media while concentrating on giving their kids a secure and nurturing upbringing.

A major component of Kutcher's life story has always been his bond with his twin brother Michael. Michael's struggles with cerebral palsy and his heart transplant had a profound impact on Kutcher's empathy and fortitude. Speaking in public, Kutcher discussed how his brother's illness impacted his life and gave him a desire to give back. His charitable endeavors, especially in the fields of health and child welfare, have been greatly inspired by this personal experience.

Kutcher is well-known for his interests and pastimes outside of acting and business, in addition to his family life. He is an avid sports fan, with a special interest in collegiate basketball and football. He frequently appears to be cheering on his favorite teams, the Chicago Bears and the Iowa Hawkeyes. In addition, Kutcher has a strong interest in innovation and technology, as seen by his investments in several tech businesses and his involvement in tech events and conferences.

Kutcher's commitment to lifelong study and self-improvement is evident in his personal life as well. He has openly expressed his passion for several things, including martial arts, which he performs regularly. His work activities reflect this quest for personal development, as he is always looking for fresh challenges and chances to broaden his horizons.

Ashton Kutcher

In his personal life, Kutcher is renowned for having a kind and approachable demeanor. He still keeps in close contact with his native friends and family despite his fame. He frequently makes his way back to Iowa, where he supports regional issues and participates in local community events. Many people find him endearing because of his grounded nature and strong connection to his roots.

Kutcher has encountered controversy in his personal life. He has been the subject of media attention and public scrutiny for several reasons, including his financial dealings and relationships. Nonetheless, he has continuously shown resiliency and a dedication to taking lessons from his mistakes. He tackles problems with a realistic and upbeat attitude, which has enabled him to successfully negotiate the difficulties of living in the spotlight.

All things considered, Ashton Kutcher's personal life is evidence of his complex nature and ability to strike a balance between his personal and professional obligations. His path from an Iowan small-town lad to a prosperous actor, businessman, and philanthropist is characterized by a strong sense of familial ties, empathy, and a desire to change the world for the better. Kutcher never stops motivating and influencing others around him, whether it is through his charitable work, his investments in tech businesses, or his appearances in movies and television.

Public Image and Presence in the Media

Throughout his career, Ashton Kutcher's public persona and media presence have played a crucial role in building his reputation as a skilled performer, astute businessman, and devoted philanthropist. He rose from a small-town Iowan to become a well-known personality throughout the world thanks to his ability to handle the pressures of celebrity without losing his personable and grounded persona.

Ashton Kutcher

After breaking out as a model, Kutcher became well-known for his portrayal of Michael Kelso in the popular television series "That '70s Show." His portrayal of the endearing but dimwitted character won him over fans and helped him become well-known. Kutcher's early success established him as a humorous actor, and his attractiveness and charm added to his appeal, especially with younger audiences. In addition to launching his acting career, his performance on "That '70s Show" paved the way for his subsequent TV and movie projects.

As Kutcher made the switch to the movie industry, he landed several parts that demonstrated his versatility as an actor. Kutcher showed his versatility by playing somber roles in movies like "The Butterfly Effect" and romantic comedies like "Just Married" and "No Strings Attached." His openness to trying out new roles and genres contributed to his popularity and solid Hollywood reputation.

Ashton Kutcher

After creating and hosting the MTV prank show "Punk'd," Kutcher's profile in the media grew dramatically. "Punk'd" gained notoriety for its intricate practical tricks on famous people. The popularity of the show not only increased Kutcher's profile but also highlighted his originality and spirit of entrepreneurship. "Punk'd" showcased his abilities as a producer and content creator while reaffirming his reputation as a naughty, fun-loving guy.

Apart from his roles in acting and producing, Kutcher's social media activity has had a significant impact on his public persona. He was among the first users of Twitter, and he rose to prominence very fast as one of the most popular personalities there. Kutcher's use of Twitter stood out due to his sincerity and open communication with followers. He frequently participated in debates on a range of subjects, provided personal perspectives, and advertised his enterprises. Through his astute use of social media, he was able to establish a sizable online following and have open lines of communication with his audience.

Ashton Kutcher

One more aspect of Kutcher's public persona is his association with the tech sector. He has been outspoken in his support of disruptive technology and creative businesses as an investor and businessman. His investments in businesses such as Uber, Spotify, and Airbnb have attracted a lot of attention, establishing him as an innovative investor. Kutcher frequently takes part in panels and tech conferences where he discusses entrepreneurship, technology, and investing techniques. The fact that he can navigate both the entertainment and technological domains has added to his complex public character.

He has further molded his public persona through his charitable endeavors, especially through Thorn. Kutcher's use of technology to fight child abuse and human trafficking is an example of his dedication to using his platform for social good. Outside of the entertainment world, he has gained respect and affection for his fervent advocacy and public speaking on these causes. The media extensively covered his 2017 appearance before Congress, during which he addressed the work of Thorn and the role that technology plays in preventing human trafficking. This testimony demonstrated his commitment to this cause.

In addition to his public persona, Kutcher's private life has garnered a lot of attention. A lot of media attention has been paid to his relationships, especially his marriages to Demi Moore and Mila Kunis. Despite the attention, Kutcher has been able to keep his family life quite quiet and grounded. Many people have come to like him because of his candor regarding his personal experiences, especially the joys and hardships of fatherhood. The media frequently highlights his long-lasting love and partnership with Kunis, with whom he shares a lengthy history dating back to their time on "That '70s Show," as a tale of enduring love and commitment.

Through a variety of ventures and channels, Kutcher has continued to increase his media presence in recent years. He is a frequent guest on talk shows and podcasts, where he shares his opinions on social and political problems as well as his career and investing strategies. Throughout these appearances, his thoughtful and articulate demeanor highlights his transformation from a comic performer to a complex public figure with a wide range of interests and contributions.

Maintaining Kutcher's media presence has been largely dependent on his capacity for self-reinvention and adaptation. He has continued to be important and relevant through his acting career, business endeavors, charitable endeavors, and social media insights. He has been able to negotiate the always-shifting terrain of celebrity and public opinion because he is open to new opportunities and willing to take calculated risks.

Overall, a combination of charisma, intelligence, and genuineness define Ashton Kutcher's public persona and media presence. His accomplishments in a variety of industries, including technology, entertainment, and philanthropy, are a testament to his wide range of skills and passions. Kutcher has created an enduring and

Ashton Kutcher

significant presence in the public eye by remaining loyal
to himself and constantly changing, inspiring admirers
and following all around the world.

CONCLUSION

Ashton Kutcher's extraordinary adaptability and unwavering desire are demonstrated by his journey from a small-town lad in Cedar Rapids, Iowa, to a globally famous actor, entrepreneur, and philanthropist. He has demonstrated over the years that he is a visionary with a strong dedication to innovation, social impact, and personal development in addition to being a charming face on television.

Kutcher's diverse public presence was shaped by his standout performances in films and television throughout his acting career. From the hilarious genius of Michael Kelso in "That '70s Show" to his audacious ventures into tragic parts, Kutcher displayed a variety of skills that won over fans all over the world. His ability to connect with people both on and off screen contributed to his

popularity as an entertainer in addition to his
performances.

After making the switch from acting to entrepreneurship,
Kutcher showed that she had a sharp business sense and
a vision for game-changing innovations. His investments
in businesses like Spotify, Uber, and Airbnb demonstrate
his commitment to fostering disruptive ideas and a
forward-thinking outlook. In addition to accumulating a
substantial fortune, Kutcher has influenced the future of
tech startups by encouraging a culture of innovation and
taking calculated risks through his venture capital firm,
A-Grade Investments.

What makes Kutcher unique, though, is his unwavering
dedication to philanthropy. He has fought against human
trafficking and child exploitation by co-founding Thorn:
Digital Defenders of Children and using technology to
defend the weak. His fervent support and active
participation in Thorn's work demonstrate his
commitment to changing the world in a meaningful way.
In addition to education, health, and environmental

sustainability, Kutcher has continuously used his resources and influence to promote positive change in these fields.

Kutcher's private life, particularly his family and relationships, has greatly influenced how the world perceives him. His ideals of privacy, family, and stability are highlighted by his marriage to Mila Kunis, their shared existence, and their dedication to raising their kids away from the constant scrutiny of the media. His life experiences—especially the ones that involved his twin brother Michael—have given him a strong sense of empathy and fortitude, which has further fueled his charitable initiatives.

To put it simply, Ashton Kutcher is the epitome of the modern Renaissance man. A guy driven by passion and purpose is depicted by his ability to succeed in a variety of disciplines, his smart use of his platform for advocacy, and his unwavering pursuit of both professional and personal improvement. His story serves as a potent reminder that success is about using one's abilities and opportunities to change the world, not just about gaining notoriety and wealth.

As Kutcher develops and takes on new challenges, his tale serves as an encouraging illustration of how commitment, creativity, and compassion can come together to leave a legacy that goes beyond the confines of a particular profession. Ashton Kutcher's accomplishments in entertainment, technology, and philanthropy are part of a larger story that celebrates progress, hope, and the resilience of the human spirit.